This Book Belongs To:

Printed in Great Britain
by Amazon

28574862R00068